Have You Ever?

Written by Tasha Pym
Illustrated by Antony Elworthy

Collins

Have you ever seen a sneep?

Have you ever heard a horp?

Have you ever touched a tiffler?

Have you ever smelt a smorp?

Have you ever tasted thoo?

A story map

:paw: Ideas for guided reading :paw:

Learning objectives: extend vocabulary exploring the meanings and sounds of new words; know that print carries meaning and in English is read from left to right and top to bottom; retell narrative in the correct sequence, drawing on the language patterns of stories; recognise common digraphs

Curriculum links: Creative Development : Explore colour, texture, shape, form and space in two and three dimensions;

Respond in a variety of ways to what they see, hear, smell, touch and taste.

High frequency words: have, you, seen

Interest words: sneep, horp, tiffler, smorp, thoo

Resources: yes and no cards, materials for drawing and modelling

Word count: 33

Getting started

- Play a game of *Have you ever?* by asking the children imaginative questions about what they have done e.g. *Have you ever combed an elephant's tail?* The child chooses a card which has *yes* or *no* on it and others have to decide whether they believe the answer to be true. The child then tells the group if it is true or not.

- Look at the cover and decide which is the title and which is the author's or illustrator's name.

- Read the title together pointing to the words.

- Read p1 and then leaf through book, discussing the pictures.

- Try to guess the names of strange creatures and plants.

Reading and responding

- Read the book together pointing to the words.

- Help the children to sound out the unusual names of the creatures and plants. Explain that they are made-up words.